LET'S CELEBRATE AMERICA

YELLOWSTONE

America's First National Park

by Joanne Mattern

RED CHAIR
·PRESS·

Let's Celebrate America is produced and published by Red Chair Press:

Red Chair Press LLC   PO Box 333   South Egremont, MA 01258-0333

www.redchairpress.com

About the Author

Joanne Mattern is a former editor and the author of nearly 350 books for children and teens. She began writing when she was a little girl and just never stopped! Joanne loves nonfiction because she enjoys bringing history and science topics to life and showing young readers that nonfiction is full of compelling stories! Joanne lives in New York State with her husband, four children, and several pets.

Publisher's Cataloging-In-Publication Data

Names: Mattern, Joanne, 1963–

Title: Yellowstone : America's first national park / by Joanne Mattern.

Description: South Egremont, MA : Red Chair Press, [2017] | Series: Let's celebrate America | Interest age level: 008-012. | Includes a glossary and references for additional reading. | "Core content classroom."--Cover. | Includes bibliographical references and index. | Summary: "As the flagship of the National Park Service, Yellowstone National Park has a special place in the hearts and minds of conservationists. It's all thanks to the leadership of far-sighted President Ulysses S. Grant and adventurer President Theodore Roosevelt. Today we can enjoy nature as it was in the early days of our nation."--Provided by publisher.

Identifiers: LCCN 2016954991 | ISBN 978-1-63440-220-0 (library hardcover) | ISBN 978-1-63440-230-9 (paperback) | ISBN 978-1-63440-240-8 (ebook)

Subjects: LCSH: Yellowstone National Park--Juvenile literature. | National parks and reserves--United States--Juvenile literature. | CYAC: Yellowstone National Park. | National parks and reserves--United States.

Classification: LCC F722 .M38 2017 (print) | LCC F722 (ebook) | DDC 978.7/52--dc23

Photo credits: p. 21, 25, 31: Dreamstime; p. 18, 19: National Park Service; p. cover, 1, 3, 4, 5, 6, 7, 8, 9, 10, 11, 12, 14, 15, 16, 17, 20, 22, 23, 24, 25, 26, 27, 28, 29, back cover: Shutterstock

Printed in the United States of America

0517 1P WRZF17

Table of Contents

The First National Park

There is a special place tucked into the northwest corner of Wyoming. This natural wonderland includes **geysers** and **hot springs**. It has towering pine forests and rushing streams. Huge bison and noisy woodpeckers make their homes here. Visitors can hike through the forests or ride a horse along the trails. They can see many amazing natural wonders.

Yellowstone is part of the United States **National Park** system. National parks do not belong to one person. They belong to everyone. Yellowstone was the very first national park.

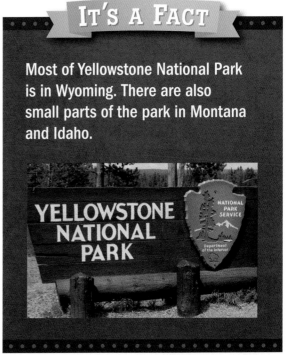

IT'S A FACT

Most of Yellowstone National Park is in Wyoming. There are also small parts of the park in Montana and Idaho.

YELLOWSTONE NATIONAL PARK

Natural Beauty

Yellowstone got its name from the Yellowstone River, which flows through the park. The river is surrounded by yellow sandstone bluffs. Native Americans in the area called the river "Mi tsi a-da-zi," which means "Rock Yellow River." French fur trappers translated the name to "Yellow Stone."

The Yellowstone River is the largest and most important river of the park.

The Yellowstone River flows through four **canyons**. One of the most beautiful is called the Grand Canyon of the Yellowstone. It is located in the eastern part of the park. The Grand Canyon of the Yellowstone is 20 miles long and up to 1,200 feet deep. The canyon was carved out by the river over millions of years. The canyon includes two waterfalls. The larger waterfall is called the Lower Falls of the Yellowstone. It falls 308 feet down into the canyon.

Yellowstone National Park covers 3,472 square miles of wilderness. That's bigger than the states of Delaware and Rhode Island put together! The park is on a high, flat **plateau**. Mountains surround it on all sides. The park includes more than 1,000 miles of backcountry trails. It would take years for someone to see everything the park has to offer.

IT'S A FACT

The Lower Falls is almost twice as high as Niagara Falls.

7

Geysers and Hot Springs

One of the most amazing features of Yellowstone is its hot springs and geysers. Both of these features form when water and steam build up underground, then burst through the surface of the Earth's crust. Yellowstone has so many geysers and hot springs because the park sits on a sea of molten rock just a few miles below the surface.

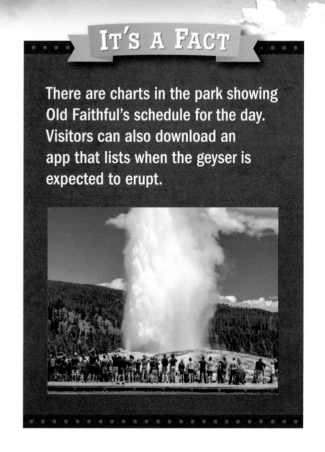

Geysers are fountains of hot water and steam. There are more than 300 geysers in Yellowstone. The most famous one is named Old Faithful. Most geysers erupt once in a while, but Old Faithful erupts on a schedule. The geyser usually erupts every 60-120 minutes. It shoots hot water and steam more than 100 feet in the air. Each eruption lasts between one-and-a-half and five minutes.

Yellowstone is also home to the largest geyser in the world. This feature is named Steamboat Geyser. It does not **erupt** very often, but when it does, it shoots water up to 400 feet high.

Steamboat Geyser is the world's tallest currently-active geyser.

Yellowstone also has many hot springs. Hot springs form when superheated water seeps out of the ground. The water collects in pools or bubbling springs. Because the rock under the water has many holes in it, the water cools, sinks into the rocks, heats up, and rises back to the surface in a never-ending cycle.

The Grand Prismatic Spring in Yellowstone National Park is the largest hot spring in the United States.

Sometimes the water from hot springs mixes with dirt. When this happens, it creates a *mud pot*. The mud boils and bubbles like hot food on a stove. Some mud pots are very colorful because of minerals in the soil. These features are called paint pots. Other mud pots smell like rotten eggs because of hydrogen sulfide gas in the water.

A *fumarole* is a different kind of hot spring. Fumaroles form when the hot water under the ground boils away before it reaches the surface. Instead of water, all that is left is a hissing column of steam.

Fumaroles can reach temperatures as high as 280°F (138°C).

A Lake from a Volcano

The Yellowstone area actually sits on a volcano. This volcano erupted about two million years ago. It erupted again about 700,000 years later. The last eruption was about 640,000 years ago. These eruptions blew rocks out of the area and created rivers of lava that flowed for thousands of years.

The eruptions blew away so much rock and dirt that it created a bowl-shaped landform called a *caldera*. Over the years, the caldera filled with water and turned into a lake. Today, people fish in Yellowstone Lake. They can also take guided boat tours around the lake.

The Yellowstone volcano is still active, but scientists do not think it will erupt again any time soon. However, the area does have earthquakes and landslides because of all the activity going on under the ground.

IT'S A FACT

Because there's a large volcano heating things up beneath Yellowstone, half the world's hot water geysers are here. In 2010, there were 3,200 earthquakes in the park. Most are small, but all are watched closely, just in case! The last time the super volcano in Yellowstone erupted 640,000 years ago, the area that's now eastern South Dakota was covered in 12 inches of ash!

Land of Fossils

There are many **fossils** in Yellowstone National Park. Some of the most amazing are **petrified** trees. Trees become petrified when minerals replace the wood and they actually turn to stone. Yellowstone is home to the greatest number of petrified trees in the world. These trees were petrified when long-ago volcanic eruptions covered them with ash. The heat and ash **preserved** the trees.

Ancient fossilized tree trunks
in the Lamar Valley

Many petrified trees are found in a place called Specimen Ridge. It is the largest petrified forest in the world. More than 100 species of plant fossils are found here.

In the northeast part of the park, visitors can see a petrified redwood tree. While other parts of the park have petrified trees in groups, this tree stands alone. All the other trees around it were destroyed by the volcanic eruption, but somehow this one remained standing.

Yellowstone's Early Visitors

Native Americans were the first people to live in the area that is now Yellowstone National Park. It is thought the first group of natives arrived about 14,000 years ago. Around the year 1400, a group of Shoshone Indians moved into the area. They lived there for 400 years.

In 1806, a man named John Colter was exploring the western lands that had recently become part of the United States. He wandered into the Yellowstone area and could not believe his eyes! When Colter returned home, he told people about the geysers and hot springs. He also talked about the mountains and forests and the many different animals living there. His tales were so strange that most people did not believe him.

Later, fur trappers moved into the area. They were looking for animals like beavers and mink to trap so they could sell their fur. These fur trappers also told others about the amazing features in the Yellowstone area. Like John Colter, most of these men were accused of lying or making up stories.

The North American mink is valued for its soft fur. The fur is covered by oily hair that is waterproof.

Fur trapper Joe Meek wrote:

"Behold! The whole country beyond was smoking with vapor from boiling springs; and burning with gases issuing from small craters, each of which was emitting a sharp, whistling sound."

Yellowstone Becomes a Park

Ferdinand Hayden

The Yellowstone area was so **rugged** it was hard to explore. By the 1870s, it was one of the last unexplored parts of the United States. In 1871, Ferdinand Hayden, the director of the U.S. Geological Survey, visited Yellowstone. He took a painter and a photographer with him. Their beautiful pictures finally proved just how amazing Yellowstone was.

The government was impressed by Hayden's work. On March 1, 1872, President Ulysses S. Grant signed a bill that preserved 2.2 million acres of land. No one could develop the land. It had to stay in its natural state, "set apart as a public park or pleasuring ground for the benefit and enjoyment of the people." With this bill, Yellowstone became the nation's first national park.

Yet, being a national park did not protect Yellowstone. Hunters and trappers went onto the land and killed many animals. Visitors damaged the wilderness as well. The park needed more protection. In 1886, the government sent in soldiers to patrol it.

The National Park Service was created in 1916. Soon afterward, it took over Yellowstone National Park. Instead of soldiers, park **rangers** now patrolled the area and kept it safe.

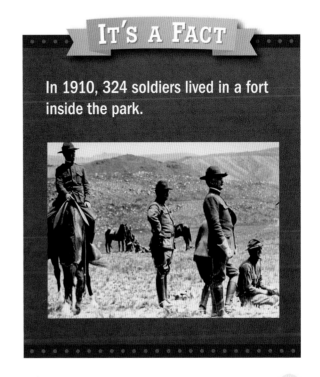

IT'S A FACT

In 1910, 324 soldiers lived in a fort inside the park.

Plant Life

Many different plants live in Yellowstone National Park. In spring, small flowers fill the fields and valleys. These include yellowbells, yellow violets, columbine, and blue flax. These flowers, and many others, are pretty to look at, but they cannot be picked. It is against the law to pick wildflowers in Yellowstone National Park.

Many kinds of berries also grow in the park. Some, like huckleberries, are good to eat. Others, like baneberries, are poisonous. Many mushrooms, both poisonous and nonpoisonous, also grow in the park. One of the most interesting is the puffball. These round, white mushrooms can be as big as a child's head!

The shores of Yellowstone's lakes are lined with trees. Water lilies and other plants grow in the water. Shrubs, bushes, and many different kind of trees rise up along the mountain slopes.

Huckleberries are small and round and look like large dark blueberries.

Fire!

One of the most common pine trees in Yellowstone is the *lodgepole pine*. Thick forests of these tall trees cover large areas of the park. For years, these trees grew without anything to stop them. Then, in the summer of 1988, lightning struck several trees in the park. The trees and bushes were very dry, and they quickly caught fire. The wildfire spread so quickly that no one could stop it. By September, more than a third of Yellowstone, or 1,250 square miles, had burned. The fires ended only when an early September snowfall put them out.

Fire rages in Antelope Creek.

A pine forest showing new growth after a forest fire that burned many trees years ago.

Many people were upset about the wildfires, but scientists explained that fire was a natural part of the park's life cycle. The lodgepole pines needed the fires to create new trees. Lodgepole pine cones are very tough and hard to open. The heat of a fire causes the cones to pop open and release their seeds. These seeds grow into new trees. By 1995, less than ten years after the fire, large areas of forests were already growing back.

Animals of the Park

Many animals live in Yellowstone National Park. The park is full of large animals, such as grizzly bears, black bears, wolves, and bobcats. Smaller mammals include foxes, weasels, deer mice, and ground squirrels.

Yellowstone is also home to animals such as bison, elk, deer, and moose. It is common to see large herds of bison and elk roaming the fields. Bighorn sheep live in the rocky and rugged mountains.

An estimated 150 grizzly bears live in Yellowstone National Park.

Birds fill the forests and fields of this national park. Large birds include bald eagles and hawks. The fields are also filled with songbirds and woodpeckers. Yellowstone's lakes and streams are filled with fish, including trout. Reptiles such as lizards and snakes live in the park as well.

The bull snake is one of six reptile species and the largest species found in the park.

Bald eagles are one of more than a dozen raptor species in Yellowstone.

IT'S A FACT

In the past, bears were a problem in the park because visitors often fed them or left garbage that the bears would eat. Rangers cleaned up the park and moved many of the bears to **backcountry** areas so they would not bother people.

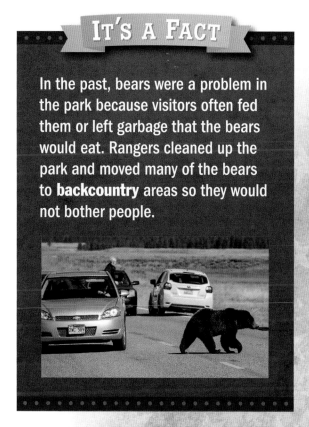

Wolves prefer to live in packs or groups. In 2016, there were about 12 packs identified in the park. 25% of the wolves wear radio collars so they can be tracked.

There are about 500 wolves in the greater Yellowstone ecosystem.

Yellowstone used to be full of gray wolves. These animals live in packs led by an **alpha** male and alpha female. Over time, visitors became afraid of the large packs of gray wolves in the park. Many of the wolves were killed. Others were trapped and moved to other places outside of the park. Because of these actions, the wolves in Yellowstone disappeared.

Not having wolves led to some big problems. Because there were no wolves to act as **predators**, the population of **prey** animals, such as elk and deer, soon became too big. There wasn't enough grass to feed so many animals. At the same time, the gray wolf was named an **endangered** species. Yellowstone would be a protected place for wolf packs to live.

In 1995, a few gray wolves were introduced back to Yellowstone. Today there are about 500 wolves living in the park and surrounding areas. Lucky visitors may hear them howling at night!

Visiting Yellowstone

More than four million people visit Yellowstone National Park each year. Most visitors come between the months of May and September. During these months, the park is very crowded. Other people visit during the winter, when it is quieter.

The Grand Prismatic Spring is one of Yellowstone's most popular attractions. It can be explored in a variety of ways including the 0.8-mile boardwalk loop.

There are five visitor centers in the park. Here people can get information, sign up for tours, and see exhibits about the park. Some visitors stay in a hotel called the Old Faithful Inn. The Inn is more than 100 years old!

Park rangers guide visitors around the park. They give talks and educate visitors about the park's history, its animals, and the amazing natural sites there. Rangers also keep park visitors safe.

Many people camp in Yellowstone. Others take long hikes, while some people just visit for the day. In the winter, people can cross-country ski or walk across the snow on snowshoes. Many visitors drive around the park on a road called the Grand Loop. The Grand Loop is 142 miles long and takes about four hours to drive.

On the Grand Loop, there are many visitor centers, museums, boardwalks, and scenic side roads.

Glossary

alpha: dominant

backcountry: an area away from populated areas

canyons: deep, narrow river valleys with steep sides

endangered: at risk of dying out completely

erupt: to shoot up in the air

fossils: the remains of ancient organisms that are preserved in rock

geyser: a fountain of hot water and steam

hot springs: flowing water that has been heated by magma beneath the Earth's surface

national park: an area that is owned and managed by the government

petrified: changed into a stone-like substance

plateau: a high, flat piece of land

predators: animals that hunt other animals for food

preserved: saved

prey: animals that are hunted by other animals for food

ranger: a person who works in a national park

rugged: rough, rocky or uneven

Learn More in the Library

Books

Holland, Ilona E. *Buddy Bison's Yellowstone Adventure*. National Geographic Children's Books, 2016.

McHugh, Erin. *National Parks: A Kid's Guide to America's Parks, Monuments and Landmarks*. Black Dog and Leventhal, 2012.

National Geographic Kids. *National Parks Guide U.S.A.* (Centennial Edition). National Geographic Children's Books, 2016.

Web Sites

National Park Service site for Yellowstone
https://www.nps.gov/yell/index.htm

Background and photos from Yellowstone
www.yellowstonenationalpark.com

Index